NUDE BLUE

KELVIN C. BIAS

ARCHIVE ZERO | NEW YORK | 2024
www.archivezero.com

Published by Archive Zero, LLC
Hardback ISBN: 978-1-955722-12-4
Paperback ISBN: 978-1-955722-13-1
E-book ISBN: 978-1-955722-14-8

Cover design by Robson Garcia Jr.
Cover photo by Kelvin C. Bias
Formatting by Polgarus Studio

for all the lovers

CONTENTS

NUDE BLUE

BLUE JEANS

"Those jeans are perfect."
He heard the voice,
Before he saw her hair.
Brown, full, like 1975.
Somewhere on the
Upper West Side.
Maybe the last
Phone booth
In Manhattan.
A liberal woman
He was certain.
He glanced young,
Still new to the city,
Its bounties uncollected.
He wondered if
She had a name.
Didn't bother to ask,
Shy, uncorrupted.
Any line would've done.
A rendezvous in a
Musky apartment.
Their blue denim matched.
Flipped a switch,
She could have
Tried him on.

RUSHING

My timber rearranges with
Little effort, downhill
Toward an odd ocean
Filled by curiosity, love,
Tangible figments of
Two imaginations.

I am your river,
Rushing, flowing,
Virule, a vent
Of liberated verve.
Our forest holds
The tallest tree.

IF YOU ASK, I'LL SAY YES

15th floor, 10th floor, 31st floor.
Cities, dots on a digital void,
Destined for a rendezvous.
The glances, the brushed
Hands, whispers: untold.
A long-ago dream
On the bathroom floor.
Always on the go,
Past the prime chance.
Post a yellow sign on the tile.
We gushed a tad too much.
Eyes, an explosion,
A willing congregation,
A breath among breaths.
If you ask, I'll say yes.

SELF-EXPERIMENTS IN CHEMISTRY

I can take off my own clothes.
Thank you very much.
The arms stretch,
The legs combine,
The lustful sighs echo
From competing windows.
The listening night,
The ghosts of ecstasies spent,
And the reunion of saints,
We are all connected.

AWAKEN

Light creeps.
Tensions release.
Fleet feet stick
To a thrilled bed.
Awaken, glisten,
The gates of eternity
Flood the streets.
The doves serenade,
While sweepers
Mold to automobiles,
Freaks parked in
Unsung shapes, as
The city sleeps.

RIFFRAFF

Two bodies, torn to pieces.
Ravenous winds whip
Desirous skin into
Desiccated red fragments,
Deeper than autumn leaves.
Rhythm bends to oblivion
Because we are vessels
For others' rise to power:
Discounted riffraff, burning,
Flung aside by the masses,
And stomped upon
Like cigarette butts.
But again, at first lightly,
The howls return, an
Atomic scent churns,
The electrified hum of
Beautiful defiance, and
We form friction, fire,
Fascination — destined
To become our own rulers,
Brighter than those who
Thought they'd conquered.
They know us not, and
They do not burn. We do,
Then we come together,
Fused by an atmospheric glue,
And ascend to Utopia,
The tallest of happy trees.

INTENSITY

How long can I wait?
(The ecstatic
Experience we
Can no longer deny.)
As long as it takes.
Water, pineapple juice,
Fuels for our combustion,
Bodies like oil.

The panting aftermath,
A guided tour of bliss.
We slide into the day,
Past tomorrow, and
Into the sunset beyond.
The end is nowhere near.
It is a pylon beyond time
While our intensity burns.

PRIVILEGE

Everyone should wag their tongues.
Be dogs in rhythm for
The privilege of living.
Passion, redolent action,
Part of the bastion
Of time, faith, love,
Immortal lips, predestination.
Enjoy the sea, the roiling chaos,
For undulating waves make
For better instigation.

SQUEEZE

The harder I squeeze,
The juicier things get.
Fruits of labor,
Body parts, tin cans,
Oranges, lemons,
Chamomile planned,
A playful adventure
Shaped by golden hands.
Straddled by joy,
Shaken and stirred,
We bend but don't break,
Soft on top,
Firm bottomed.
Every part of the endeavor,
Bounce, ride, massage.
The greed of the world
Cannot defeat this motion,
This dance of fate and fluid.
Tell me where to press.

WHITE BLOUSE

I wish your white blouse
Floated to the floor,
In a pile without regard
To its style, fit, or
Place of repose.
I wish your red lips
Melted into mine and
Sequestered in a
Quiet room at
Our own speed.
I wish the chords,
The sweet melodies,
Floated evermore
In synch with the
Electricity of a
Moonlit night in Tokyo.
I wish the midnight
Portal to liquid
Dreams filled my
Soul with memories,
The kind too risqué
To fade into the darkness.
I wish the rhythmic patter
Continued for all to hear,
For all to see, for all
To admire. Jealousy,

A fleeing thief in the
Wee hours of a neon
Rendezvous: I wish.

CRIMSON

"Come in," she sighed,
An unseen woman,
From the darkest gloom.
I imagined she
Wore a sequined
Mask — the kind
Worn at a ball —
And nothing else.
But maybe I
Protected my heart,
Merely projected.
The room, pitch,
Smelled of books.
Nothing visible
On the spectrum,
Except the tiniest
Sliver of light
Beneath an iron door.
We were in a mansion
Somewhere in the hills,
Like something
J.G. Ballard imagined.
Drips of expectation
Melted the cold air.
"The switch is near
The dying light."

I turned, mesmerized,
Stumbled, then
Gained my stride,
A hypnotic beat
Dressed in time.
When I found
The illumination
Device, I cried.
Tears of anticipation,
Yet I breached
The unknown with
My delirious flick.
Suddenly, I
Inhabited a
Crimson room.
The walls, floor,
Ceiling—there were
No windows—and
A chandelier, equal
Partners in
Blood-colored union.
She sat in a
Matching chair,
Wearing her
Same-hued gown:
A skeleton.
"Kiss me." Her
Hand reached
Toward mine.
I gripped;
Curiosity won.

I obliged and
The gown
Transformed.
Red fibers,
Now flesh,
An ecstatic
Release,
Coalesced
Onto her spine.
"Again, sublime."
My lips met her
Ossified chin.
More flesh,
More skin,
More kisses.
My eager garments
Joined the charge.
Threads from my sleeve,
And soon, too, I was bare.
Continued titillations,
Ensnared by touch,
She was nearly complete.
Breasts, legs, arms,
Hips, curves, and
Melodies, akin
To Old West bandits
And their fire-
Making ilk.
"Rise with me," she said,
And took my hand.
We walked for

Hours in the garden,
Stars in earthly content.
No shame, or testament.
Only the memory
Of a deep purple
Sunset emerged
From the room
On the hill
That no longer existed.
We looked into the sky,
We bled into one,
Then kissed the
Sanguine moon.

BACKLIT

The dark form
Emits sin…or is
That in the mind
Of the beholder?
Her curves offer
Themselves to
Dalliances within
A kinked cerebellum.
Astride a doorway,
The light creates
Silk paths to an
Erotic dimension.
Wattage and winks,
Decorum slinks into
The shadows, happily.
There are no arguments,
There are no harsh words.
Only a silhouette.
Her mystery is beyond
Pure: she is desire.

JULY

Death, that vagabond cut,
Like your body in July.
Globes warmed,
Inclines traversed,
I braved summer waves
To reach this hottest shore.
We will live until the
Day after never.
California vibes kept
Tops down and bikinis small.
The wind whipped past
The yellow Corvette.
You and I pressed
Into action. Lipids,
We looked up
At the conniving sun,
And shed clothes
In a Santa Barbara bungalow.

ALL THOSE NIGHTS

All those nights,
When the stars fell,
When you
Beckoned
The calls.
My sacred
Addiction,
Up marble halls,
Down on your
Thrill. The fiery
Carpet, thick,
Your red robe,
The willing chair.
I'll cry at eternity.
Molten devotion,
Dream after dream,
When we fulfilled
Each other's
Urges. Hands,
Fingers, tongues,
Instruments of
The long nocturne,
Bare skin, abreast,
From happiness.
God and Goddess
Within the spin.

An eager sculptor
Made us fossils
In this forever glee.
Obsidian, true,
In tears or rain,
I am your chiseled
Supplicant born
Of your skill, a
Glamorous rendezvous.

WHENEVER

Whenever you're alone,
Give me a call, text, ring,
Craft an Email,
Type a What's App,
Dispatch a
Carrier pigeon.
Don't keystroke into
An artificially
Intelligent domain.
I have genuine words.
For your disposal,
Aspiration, rumination.
I will tell you of
Your beauty, your
Intelligence, the fire
You kindle deep
In my recesses.
The motions you
Engender in my
Limbic system.
I will build you a temple.
I will call you goddess.
I will give you the same
Salient pleasure.
As words waft and
We ooze into tomorrow.

THE DEEP MELANCHOLY OF WATCHING A *SEX AND THE CITY* EPISODE SET IN PARIS 20 YEARS LATER AS A MAN OF A CERTAIN AGE

Streets I used to walk blink across a screen.
White heels, a passing bateau on the Seine,

Pixels of the mind, memories kind and unkind,
Vicissitudes of tomorrow, distant consonants.

No sex, no charm—or unlicensed to practice—
The former days glitch, the brain recalibrates.

From New York to Paris and back again,
Like the Shire but with Blahniks, swirled.

What has this 1 a.m. episode wrought, pray tell?
Books, authors, Polish libraries. Places in name.

The grace of girlfriends, encounters to the wind.
Things remain, unfurled in my Eiffel blind.

SUNFLOWERS IN WINTER

We are golden rays,
Propitious shades,
Light curved into shapes,
Feasts bent into fuel
For the inevitable fall.
We lie, tantalized, awake,
While leaves curdle
Beyond the waning stream.
We place logs in the kiln,
Enter hot springs as
Winter's thieves die
At our gates, love
Our primed prison.
We, like ripe fruit,
Create sunflowers,
And pressed lips,
Draped in transient bliss.
To turn yellow again.

TEARS AT 4:34 A.M.

Father, can you hear me?
Can you see my tears?
Years later, they flow
Unmuted down a
Glistening cheek,
The glow of a screen
Makes bounty with
Their knowing truth.

What would you say?
If you can see, the
Country, the fallout,
The precipitation
Outside the window,
Elsewhere and inside.
The child eulogizer,
The man born of love.

PLACES TOO COLD TO
MAKE LOVE

Antarctica, we can try.
The Pyrenees, June please.
St. Germain, Frankfurt,
The last syncopated
Heaves of lungs
And limbs intertwined in
A long-ended liaison.
The blasphemous lies,
The night we spy.
How cold is your love?

TRUSTWORTHY

I won't tell your secrets.
We'll create new demons.
I won't test your illusions.
They'll blossom, no lies,
Below a libidinous sunrise.
I won't steal your soul,
That succulent legion,
Before heaven, beyond eleven.
We'll explore other regions.
I won't make you whisper.
Scream and deliver.
The trustworthy tides of treasure,
A dream, wide-eyed.
Dear, pronate without pressure.
You'll have to believe me.

BENEATH THE MANHATTAN BRIDGE DURING A THUNDERSTORM

Graffiti, clay of the creators,
Enshrines the lovers.
They clutch; they spill,
While the heavens
Release their fluid.
They, born of an ancient flow,
Kiss as cars ferry above,
Mindful of the electricity.
There are no watchers,
Only an earthworm dances
Beneath a soggy *N.Y. Times*.
This DUMBO time is theirs.
The world, ambivalent,
Yet the creatures compel
All to worship the sun.

IF IT WEREN'T FOR YOU, I'D HAVE NO DREAMS

This is no idle declaration,
No plan of seduction.
The desires are bold,
The interlude, manifold.

If it weren't for you,
I'd have no dreams:
Your scented manifestation,
Your lustful lamentation.

There would be no fantasies,
No altogether walks as
Fresh raindrops collected
On our inspired flesh.

But here, in time's fold,
We dream, grow old.
Whilst the days of youth
Become are final booth.

ABSINTHE

Green viper in a bottle,
Weigh the consequences.
The victim becomes
Conqueror, the prey,
A victim, delirious
With imaginary friends.
Fiends for love
Become raw devils,
Astride every open door.
Banned fluids and
Intuitive constitutions,
The liquid pales
In the face of pale horses.
Kiss the bottle, unwind friend.

HER

I saw her walking
Away, jeans and flips.
Her hips signaled,
My imagination piqued.
Had she thought
The same as I
Walked away,
Unaware of her gaze?
A kiss fomented,
During a daydream.
Her exquisite legs
And political leanings
Aroused my succulent
Delectations. We shared
The same atmosphere.
She gave me words,
Which served as plinths
To carnal wishes.
It's beyond my control.
I smile, willing, an
Involuntary tic.
If she touched me,
I might explode.
We would become
One shape, one
Continuous thrust,

A thirst for knowledge,
And ecstasy, beauty,
Running delirious on a
Rainy shore at dawn.
Wet with rapture,
Wet with lust,
Wet with passion,
We, goddess and god,
Stood together,
In an uncloaked universe,
Wrapped in sensual gifts.
My smile remained.

DEUS EX MACHINA

It goes without saying:
Ça va sans dire.
You are my calque,
Borrowing my body,
Your machine when
Things are unsolvable.
We are solvent
Creatures, instant
Gratification, the
Ultimate happy end.

SEX SHOP

Beads, bells, butts, and bliss.
Contraptions for your pleasure.
No one knows you here.

ROSE

The fantasies of a flower
In a foreign desert land,
Her brown skin radiant
Under the forgiving sun.

We've never made love.
Until the sand stops
In the hourglass, time
Surpassed and replaced.

Children, family, there are
Many other roses,
But none more compelling.
Even her thorns captivate.

THE NEED

You, in nothing.
A flash of brilliant skin,
Nipples, contraband,
Black hair everywhere,
Complicit traces,
Spills and stains
Against a black sofa.
As we whisper
Fulfill my naked need.
Our deed, a rocket,
A never-ending ship
Destined for our
Own ball of fire.
In a boundless universe
With unknown rules,
There is only the deed.

WORDPLAY

Words before play.
Play after words.
We are in the middle,
Uncloaked prior to the act.
How many will there be?
We need not find
The words because
We will be free.
Undaunted, unsheathed,
Performers plying words.

I AM YOURS

In the morning,
When the light
Ordains with
Outstretched beams,
Tight against sheets.
The afternoon,
When the leaves
Grow by millimeters,
Rain falls in heat,
And the sky bellows.
In the evenings,
When the sighs of
Our longings join.
I am stripped wherever,
However, whichever
Way she commands,
Unfiltered in her mind.
I am bare to the fancy
Of unbridled ingenuity.
I am wind in her tree.

EGRESS

The white river
Flows for
Everyone,
Creates
Everyone,
Imbues life
With purpose
For everyone.
We love, we
Feel, we spin.
We taste
Each other.
Blood rages,
Bodies bare,
Upright, in
Tandem motion,
Bless the floor.
We want the
Foundation,
The sacred.
The love in
A box for all
To unwrap, or
Try to steal.
We remain
Joined, firm

In the outcome:
There is only
Egress.

AWE

The wind howls
Beyond the pines,
While sheets
Tangle on a soft
Plain. Two bodies
Dazzle, one arched
Toward constellations
Beneath strands of
Moonlight. Her smile
Conquers nations,
Her rare facade
Leaves no recourse.
Mouth agape, I
Counter with a grin
Of ascribed awe.

LOVE IS A HARSH MISTRESS

Cold, banal, indifferent.
You need her, that
Bright shadow at
The precipice of
An expectant future.
The sun illuminates
Everything you want to see.
The mind hides the rest.
Love binds so long as you
Don't put her in second place.

MOLD

The black furnace grows
While memories of bliss fade.
We crave some clean love.

MY MIND IS A FERTILE PLAYGROUND OF CLASSIC LUST

I watch a silver square in the dark,
A beacon of images to fill the time.
Large-scale installations: Kiefer,
Serra, bicycles of the cerebral kind.
White dresses, sublime, in a
Seething cauldron of imagination.
These flickering pixels, snow
For the infinite shoveling.
I stack them all, peel the layers,
The folds of my cerebellum.
Then, she appears, a creature,
Displayed like purple roses
At the edge of a reflecting pool.
Am I dreaming? Asleep at the wheel?
Or miles away on a starship,
Filled with the vestiges of Earth?
The flowers are too many to count.
Their fragrance intersects with
The waft of her perfume, the plume:
She, the blessed sanctum, I, her drink.
The metaphysical chameleon,
A jukebox with every song.
The darkness is all around,

But I do not notice its clutches.
There is too much beauty,
Too much innate curiosity.
Alone in the winter of desire,
My mind is a fertile playground
Of classic lust, dust for the ages.
I can create any shape, any image.
Instead, the goddess guides me,
Ever still, breaths, fast to my lips.
Our journey of the carnal, unblind,
Even within the curling void.
The universe, my head, two crying
Children with a need to understand.
Nude, pained, bent, tempted.
She abides every whimsy for
We are stars, we are stars,
We are stars — consciousness afar.

PRESSING ZERO

Temptation seizes a number,
A place to press in the
Deepest of nights, for
Hounds of lascivious bait.
The lines are always open.
Silk voices directed for,
And by, your content.
Libidinous charms,
Comforting exits,
Zero is your friend.

THE WAYWARD FOUNTAIN

Where do the flights
Of fancy alight?
Requited love,
Or washed away
In centuries-old
Aqueducts, unbound
For Trevi Fountain?
How many lovers
Will set you free?
How many will
Lead to your death?
No matter, dear,
In the end we
All flow to the sea.

THE CEMETERY ON
THE RIDGE

Rows and rows and rows:
A resting place for crows.
Stones on the ridge,
Gray in the darkness,
Like the hulls of
Immigrants' ships.
The settlers loved their
Homeland, but came for
A new view, drank gin,
Formed more kin.
Years and years and years.
Numbers on an epitaph,
No one wanted to do the math.
Felled by the Crow, or
Another "civilized" gun:
Rage and The West.
Everyone worshiped the
Cemetery against the sun.
They gave it all their love,
Criss-crossed crosses,
And dug their own tombs.
Surrounded by the joy
Of a family of rocks.
Where every night,
Moon dials unlocked.
And ghosts made
Whoopee off the clock.

GLIMMER

The golden hour
Belies the blue hour.
The docks by the lake:
Harbor for canoes,
Kayaks, glass-bottom
Boats and sin,
Attractions to
Contemplate the
Universe. A time
For elegant sequins
Reflected in the neon
Glow of the sun's last
Emergent streaks.
Restaurant plates
Clatter, a cacophony
Of ice cream and lime.
Moments of severe fire,
The brightest on the
Horizon, a bank of
Kaleidoscopic mastery.
The glean, the glimmer,
The glow, bow to the
Ends of the shore,
A make-believe
Entity of dreams.
Summer rain
In Frankfort, as
Michigan blinks.

I'M STILL THERE

I'm still there,
In the empty rooms,
Where we once
Frolicked without
A chair. My arms,
Plinths of steel,
Bolstered by
Your nubile thrill,
The consenting fun,
The beautiful
Undulations, never
Need for furnishings.
The floorboards,
The only witnesses.
I tried to stay in this
Place, suspended
Like you, upside down.
Our lips danced
As intermingled
Limbs braced
For recognition.
We burned bright,
No clothes for miles,
Only the rumble
Of the distant train.

SHADOW HAND

My hand is
Your hand.
My fingers
Are your
Seamless lips,
Your decibels.
I am a shadow
In the dark.
A shadow of
A peeled past.

TWO STRANGERS
IN A FOREIGN LAND

The steam from the
Antiquated engine
Mined the lovers' air.
A woman, a man.
North of Eiger,
Beyond inhibition.
Two strangers
Bound for nowhere,
Beneath a smiling moon.
A 19th century excursion
In a 21st century glare.
Gadgets turned off,
Minds turned on.
Conversation flowed.
Compartment C, Car 193.
Words, glances, grins.
She, in white leather,
He, in a blue suit—
Agitators raged
Against society—
Spies of possibility,
Draped by green
Upholstery, hosiery
Visible beyond the
Edge of her skirt.

They stood, they
Admired, they
Pressed time,
Basked in Luna's
Eternal dance,
Yet theirs was
Happenstance.
No names, no regrets.
The anonymous pair
Returned to the night.
A wild kiss, followed
By heartbreak.

SEX & POETRY

Intercourse and interplay.
They flow, they bend,
Words with no need
Of meaning, words
With every interpretation,
all and none, an explosion
Of everything. Oozed
From a creative orgy.
That I find you an
Unmatched vixen: the worst
Kept secret in the universe.
I command time for you.

CCTV

Why care who watches?
Love breaks unprintable minds,
Spring's revolution.

MORNING LIGHT

Beams of radiance
Through the blinds.
The golden gradient
Gesticulates over gray.
I don't want this 'rise
Without you, together
We belong to the
Beyond, within our
Own box of salvation.
We are dreams of dreams,
Essence bathed in life.
Light of light, love
Of love, ashes of ashes,
Lust of lust. Delight.

YOUR NAME

Cries in the dark,
Sounds out and about.
Beyond the window screen:
The flow of chi,
The flow toward we.

When I'm alone
In your mind,
Forlorn in your naked sky,
I can't escape
Your name.

I CANNOT CONTINUE

Your lips, your smile,
The turned fever
Enters a welcome domain.
You release my shirt.
You continue.
You release my shoes,
My…you continue.
I am a sitting duck,
Defenseless.
You are true.
You drain me
Of my essence.
Contraband
Between your teeth.
I explode. And now…
I cannot continue.

DO YOU DREAM
EROTIC DREAMS?

I can't remember the reasons,
Only the ecstatic smile.
The smooth feel of your shell
In the unknowing void,
A river cuts a canyon.
You stand tall, bare,
My fingers there.
Your figure an apron
For a resplendent sky.
Clouds pass in an eternal
Bid to keep the moment alive.
A replay, won't let you die.

FACES IN THE DARK

"Are you coming?"
The taxi door slid open,
And I slid into love.
August, a thunderstorm
Made Manhattan thick
With lust, a street gloss that
Still resides inside.
The night lies alone,
The clothes come undone.
While myths and lions
Of lore, twist as we kiss,
Faces in the dark,
We make oceans.
No denials, solely motion,
And flesh hums.

DR. SEUSS MAKES LOVE

Zips, lips, hips, dips.

RIPPLE

Tears, or an
Army of lovers?
On one side
Of the earth
It's 2 a.m.
On the other,
Jealous day.
Upon this
Shrouded half,
We blend into
The Infinite
Void. Humans,
Intertwined.
Splayed,
Driven,
Killed,
Ravished,
Spoiled,
Syncopated.
Seeds on a
Tilting planet.
Beings of light.
Captured like
Reflections
Against the din:
Masquerading.

Traffic lights,
Sidewalks,
Slippery streets,
All pools to
Make their
Own ocean,
Our ripple
Emerges
On the other
Side of another
Pool in another
Universe. Ribald
Thoughts flush
With hope.
Rise. Burst.
Break true.
Let the rain
Fall where
It may, and
Form its own
Waterway.
As the next
Meteorite
Takes aim,
A heart
Explodes.

TREMOR

They say the earth moved,
The ladies and lords of
The television screen.
There is no evidence:
Declared by our presence
In the carnal light of union.
We fan only fearless winds
While epicenters form elsewhere.
Trees may sway, glow remains.
Cracks may form, we configure,
Pillows discarded like froth in
An overflowing glass of beer.
We don't have time for the
Jocular apocalypse.
We have other delights,
Another kite, another tremor.
The daffodils on rolling, roiled,
Hills, bend, whereas in our sector
Seeds glide on the wind, for
We are each other's movement,
A terrestrial tsunami—wave after wave—
Currents in pleasure's abyss.

THE NECKLACE

Whither or whether
We want, a prize:
A white necklace
Spent on overdrive.
You and I engaged,
Clad in blue breath.
Meanwhile, wheat
Still grows in Kansas.
Family heirlooms
Beget new families,
New loves, new stories,
Vibrations of desire
That ripple across time.
But at the end of existence,
Love is the only essence.

GREEN BIKINI

The contrast cuts the deep blue.
The fervent passion stirs,
The oiled limbs call like sin.
A navel, a toe, another elbow:
Positioned for the sun's worship.
Three green triangles adjust
To her deciduous figure.
Even the sand wonders
When they will tumble.
Two fly away, birds of prey,
Destined for immortality.
Dainty steps glisten with the heat.
She holds us all on a string.
The lethal smile engenders rapture.
Twirls, laughs, grins: toss
Everything and everyone.
As the eyes tell titillating tales,
And dueling straps stretch
At the behest of beauty,
Inhibitions fall to the ground.
The smooth groove of summer
Envelops the scene, and
The hymns of youth tiptoe
To the most distant shores.

YOURS

Your breasts are manna
Because they are yours.
Your fierce intelligence
In the face of my
Lecherous desires is
Tantamount to the
Continued power of
Your charms and
My fidelity to them
Because they are yours.
Your sharp countenance
Shines like no other
Because it is yours.
The alchemy you
Weave without alcohol
Occludes my brain
Because it is yours.
The mastery over
Your sense of place
Within the universe
Fells armies because
It is unequivocally yours.
And I lay dead on
The side of the road,
Body beautified by a nova,
Thoughts still ripe.

OUT SLEEPWALKING

There is food in the refrigerator,
Plastic containers stacked and
Armed for a 3:33 a.m. battle.
There are no victors.
A man ambles with no
Destination, only the erotic
Reveries of a relationship
Many sunrises past.
He shuffles to a bus stop,
A place of muscle memory:
The spot where the weeds grew.
Graffiti on the outskirts of
A northeastern city marked
A sad tale beneath haunting
Streetlights, he stopped
Believing long ago, but
At first light, the chance for
Charms rekindles, he awakes
In his own bed, filtered rays,
With love his new lover.

FIGMENTS

I awoke after I finished:
Nocturnal emanation,
A reality, a digression.
The logical consequence
Of her unbridled everything —
That indescribable delectation.
I wonder if she woke from
The same impetus,
As the moonlight
Faded into sunrise.
Do we seethe, good-looking,
Or are we just figments?

IN YOUR ARMS AS THE SEA THRUSTS UPON OUR BODIES

White foam lashes us,
A delirious whip from
Whence we don't want
To escape, nor to recover.

Face, tongue, lips,
We are fertility,
Viscous fun ignited
In a vast bath.

Friction and heat,
But no raw pain.
Only the rapture
Of lucid longing.

I push into your soul,
Your form, a vessel,
Sails into the same
Horizon, and time seeps.

MISTRESS ZERO

In this remote year,
Atoms and molecules
Reign in different form:
Mechanical people
Service *people*.
Terms of science,
Or superstition?
We don't care.
We want Mistress Zero.
She'll do whatever
Our pleasure demands.
The first and last model
Plots her next scheme.
Consumers dream, and the
Biological cells begin
Their game once more.

HOW LONG HAVEN'T I
BEEN TOUCHED

How long haven't I been touched.
I am a prisoner tied to a beautiful hill.
The cage of my invention
Leads to a destiny commingled with fear.

Noble thoughts plunge into icy water,
Passion cannot fathom the empty stare.
We need to be naked together,
To frolic in the playground of black hair.

How long haven't I been touched.
How long haven't I been crushed.
Tenants, bills, forgotten vows.
Like drinking milk without a cup.

Drop your robes, your concern.
Fly away on the far side of bliss,
Capture your own thoughts,
Enacting them on this poor bard.

THE BLUE DOOR

The blue door let me in.
That stalwart steed served
Boldness, my willing friend.
The address uptown,
A trip on the 1 train.
I liked to listen
To the sound of thunder
While her nightgown
Dropped to the floor,
And we mated in the chair.

SPLENDOR

The words are the thrill,
The splendor in the grass,
The splendor in the mind,
The splendor in the
Ecstatic, ever elastic,
Multitude of imagination,
Wherein all things are real.
Felt, emulsified, interjected.
The land welcomes lovers,
Where there are but smiles.

DISASTERS AT 5:11 A.M.

The curious house,
The tingling mood,
The nude silhouettes
Of two bodies in June.
We arc again and
Again and again,
Resplendent in grins.
We make noise the
Whole neighborhood
Hears, if they believe,
If the night allows.
While significant
Others quake as the
Earth moves in Japan,
There's no walk of shame,
Only the shadows of bliss.
We eat love for breakfast.

I LOVE THE NIGHT

Nobody tells me what to do.
Only you. Only in frenzy.
The commotion of pattering rain,
Slick as we slide into tomorrow.
Wet, we break bread with
Each other's limbs in contented
Contortions, lissome fixtures.
We want chaos, the sounds,
The heavens, the horizontal
Patterns on the 1979 disco floor.
There are minions who feel this way.
They groove, they stare deep
Into your eyes while the bongos play.
Rhythmic grease dances in a kitchen
On hell's frozen surface somewhere
South of 14th Street, but north of sin.
I am all these people, gin grins with you,
Destitute, 'cause I love the night.

NEGATIVES

We took pictures,
Mantel on fire,
Though black and white
Held stark domain.
You, nubile; me, shy.
Outside, the sky
Displayed pinpricks.
Settings on a camera,
Antiquated gadgets.
Nocturnal angel posed
For what end? Two birds,
Pecking at silhouettes,
Ecstasy, a bright halo,
Astride a dark room.
Throw away the negatives.
I'll never see her again.

DIVORCE

The world is your lover,
Everyone, a potential paramour.
Inhibition, clothes, sin,
They need not apply.
They do not exist.
The force of freedom,
Battles the feral wind.
If the flag is tattered,
Sew a new curtain.
Weave a new tapestry,
Free from longing,
Filled with ecstatic
Possibility. Rise, smile.
Ingest, digest, purr.
Whomever, whenever, you please.
No one will tell you no.
Sigh the most beautiful lullaby
As you hear the tambourine play,
And dance unclad in the rain
For all and no one to see.

PURPLE PIER

The seconds before
The Sun oozes into
A destined tomorrow,
Bold dolphins flip, and
Gracious delights
Overtake two hearts
At the end of the pier.
Wooden boards
Here today, drifting
In generations.
Exquisite gloss,
The horizon is
Your mirror,
A tender color
Deeper and deeper,
Regal, not venal.
The sky's purple
Lingerie, rules
Purple cars,
Purple dreams,
Purple hats at a
Thrift store in Venice
As purple people
Procreate in
A sublime dimension.
Infinite midnights,

Souls by the bay.
Prepare yourself:
Xanadu, inside
The goddess' mind.

THIS IMAGINED TRYST

This imagined tryst,
Inhabits a forest
Of the mind that
Doesn't need rain.
Refracted sunlight
Through the door,
It begins the same.
Fabrics rent
Across the threshold,
Flesh, one of many
Petals to be lay
Our earthly shapes
Amongst the erotic
Scepter of rumination,
Excitation. Ribald
Rivers bubble
From the source,
The rose, and roses
Of our joint elation.
Shower me with joy.
I lay still. Your legs
Between mine.
Interspersed,
Intertwined,
Interstellar.
We, stars, reform,

We wait,
Refreshed, and
Do it once more,
Ever a cycle,
Awash in window
Panes on the 36th floor.

MEEK

I am clay; you are the mold.
Together, pasteurized lubricant.
My shy hand drinks
Meek milk from a vat of
Submissive urges.
What will they think?
Fear dons a cape,
Sleek dresses, and
Wall Street obscenities,
Cobblestones, dawn subversion.
Like origami,
I fold to your will.

BEANSTALK

Where do your vines bend
When mine bend into you?
Leaves, light and limber —
Statistics — climb high
Into your florid air.
Beyond the green door,
Our canopy shields
Every lover for we are
Raw, viscous, lush.
Bare beneath the sun.
Corkscrewed, longer, further,
Pistil pitched and pure,
Stamen saturated.

MILK

Hold the thistle,
This dandelion
Tall in the wind.
I go where you blow,
Preferably in the sun.
Inside is fine yet
My seeds cannot grow
On the mahogany table,
Or through your
Tantalized thorns, so
Bring me closer,
Walk me to the wall,
Then take it down,
Glorious to the outside
World, bewitched by
Beautiful silks we weave
In the throngs of bliss.
We moil, we mix,
We produce infinite milk,
And gasp until sunset.

THE ROOT OF ALL EVIL

As we lie naked,
Torn against
The night,
Angels of
Restraint
Plummet
To the street.
No secrets.
Yes, I want to.
Everywhere.
You read my mind.
Please sanctify
My desires,
And leave me
A firefighter
Pitted at
The root
Of all evil.
We cannot
Be extinguished.

THE MOST BEAUTIFUL
SAD DREAM

I only remember 10 seconds.
You and I enthralled
On the bathroom floor,
Ravishing mortals,
Trapped in this mystical
Portal where parallels
Open and reality flees.
All I have now are
Pillars filled with tears
After realizing nirvana
Was over—the most
Beautiful sad dream.

IF YOU RING THE BELL

If you ring the bell,
I'll whisper you're
Fortunes, I'll
Shoot arrows
To the farthest moon.
If you touch yourself,
I'll be what you need.
If you stand firm
In the blinding
Light filtered
Through the blinds, I'll
Be your morning wax.
If you glisten and
Arise, I'll be your
Triassic beast,
Bones and all.
In this passion,
In this time,
We are immortal,
Desperate lullabies.

THE UNDRESSING

When a beautiful woman undresses you,
Time snaps, the sensation stretches into a
Zillions zones, the zenith of zig-zag zeal.
There are only lovers, beasts with no names,
Curdled on a bed in Gramercy Park, a 15th
Century castle in Rome, or a Parisian room.
The great undressing addresses all needs.
We lean against dressers, unsheathed,
Fitting into new hilts, new slices of ecstasy.
Devils do care…we make them jealous.

I'LL REMEMBER THIS MOMENT
WHEN IT RAINS

The toys beckon like a child.
There isn't much time,
Before school, before tiny
Voices edge to the threshold.
When did we disappear?
That long ago voyage,
The eggs splattered on the floor,
Remind me of the unknowing,
Which catapults us to this second.
I'll remember this moment
When it rains, when we let
The water cleanse all that exists.

TRI-X

Elbows cast shadows
At the center of the frame.
Sunlight shrieks past the fireplace.
The Bolex cranks, her body
Clutches the collective imagination.
We don't know what we have.
Fuji film captures instances,
Assurances we are alive,
Insurance for the next take.
Gray, white, and black,
The fleeting image mocks
Our memories and we yearn
For carnal magnification.
The evidence will be seen.
We'll peek around the edges,
Ready for our close-up.

SHADES OF GRAY

The image projected
On her nude figure
Was painted hours
Before, transferred while
Still dripping—the
Machine ruined—
And peach blush
Ruminated while
She waited on a
White futon. She
Spread across the
Apparatus, her
Loneliness addressed.
Strokes and symbols
Whispered with her
Gentle fingers.
She basked in
Heroic purgatory,
A revolutionary.
Symbiotic secretions
From the heavens
Ricocheted against
A distant window.
Her electric wire
Hung like an exclamation,
Signs and sighs echoed

Into the afterlife of
Daylight's glare.
In these moments
Before darkness,
She panted, she
Showered, she bathed,
She repeated numerous
Steps of passionate
Reveries, but none
Lasted longer than
The real thing, the
Heat of pressed humans.
Those dreams spiraled
In the final frame of day.

FLUTTERS

Black hair flutters
In the spotlight,
A dark floor
Delineates a
Halo for your
Exquisite voice.
A red dress dignifies
A beguiling bodice,
Testament to
Equal intelligence.
Rooms stretch,
Warp, bleed, and
We sigh in our
Own avenues
Of air-conditioned lust.

LOVECAKE

We were beautiful back then.
Took pictures when we
Fucked, lips locked,
Opinions heard, words minced,
Served with red wine.
Those sublime days reside in the mind.
Their reminiscence echoes with hope,
But languishes in a vacuum.
We need to add power,
Ply sake, make lovecake.

ANTICIPATION

Syncopation,
Or damnation?
Neither. We reach
Electrification,
Fantastical
Destination.
Our lips, antenna
Stripped of reserve,
We shatter
Anticipation.

BLUEFISH

I am a bluefish,
With you in Okinawa.
We swim in one sea.

LYING NAKED IN A HOTEL ROOM BED

The players have no names.
She's a star, in alias
And by reputation.
They work the front desk.
Make illogical requests
As the midnight clocks walks.
Soon, they will exchange
Pleasantries, clothes, fluids.
Circle the room, naked,
Jaybirds in flight, elongated,
Or otherwise displayed.
Even if she doesn't like poetry,
The words are always there.
Yelled, drawn, coughed
Into existence in a throw of bliss.
They don't care what lies they tell,
Lying on the bed in
Their birthday suits.
They share stains
And create new ones.

GLISTEN

Listen for the sound
Of the mirrors.
Resonances penetrate
The mind like
A luscious knife,
Pleasant in time.
Water, rays of light,
The joyous lampposts
Deep in your recesses
Awaken recollections.
There is mindful play.
There are structured shards
With painless edges only
Destined for infinity.
Love swirls and we
Tumble in a cool
Summer room, two
Sides of a surface.
I, the happiest glisten
In the land of dreams.

SWAYING

You are the wind.
Branches, leaves,
Blades of grass,
Bend like lovers.
Faces face your
Perfection, the
Gentle soul
Jangling keys
To the universe.
Everyone in awe,
Everyone attentive,
Beauty in the swaying.

JOHNNY'S BEASTS

The tattoo revealed nothing.
Johnny's Beasts: square
Across her breasts.
The cigarette smoke,
Ripe in the dingy air,
Told me more. The danger
Hung there, like smog in summer.
The air-conditioned "exotic" bar—
Girls, girls, girls in neon—
Somewhere past Hotel California.
A desert mouse peed in the corner.
The rock ballad bit all comers.
There were only us three,
Each gaming for gratification.
She bent on four limbs,
As her lips mesmerized
The spot where her heels
Dug in time after time.
She rose, in splendor,
Everything on view.
Beautiful, if not for
The black ink and taboo.
Biker Bill and mystery man,
Maybe the Johnny in question,
Both drunk, like me, in
The midst of a strobe light

Reverie, with tassels and frills.
We eyed one another, just her and I,
Made love 1,000 times
In the flash of a thunderbolt.
Fuck Johnny,
I'll never be here again.

HER BEAUTY
SWALLOWED THE SUN

Her beauty swallowed the sun.
Her fingers stole rays like
A bandit from another dimension.
She breathed different air.
She filled the sands of time
In everyone's mind.
They said Apollo cast her away
Out of jealousy, body bad,
The slang definition.
A muse for legions of artists,
Don't stand beside her,
There's too much hydrogen.
Water unquenched thirst.
She reflected the infinite beach
Until the day she evaporated.

TIJUANA

It was the type of
Dress that elicits
Drunken texts
At 1:27 a.m.
"You're a
beautiful goddess…"
The truth: nothing
But the facts ma'am.
Bosoms bold while
Boisterous cheers
Denuded fantasy.
Black hair and cloth,
Lithe legs, blessed.
Empowered by
A single word
Draped across dreams:
Tijuana. Somewhere,
Bibles cry in a motel.

BEADING

Sweat beading,
Dreamers beaming,
The waterfalls of
Color cascade from
Bourbon Street balconies.
Eyes and ears afire,
Minds and bodies
Engage in required desire.
Purple sunsets in
Each orb of a necklace
Represent this time,
This always memory.
And the people left behind:
Polished fiends.

CURVES AHEAD

She stood on the corner
Of seduction and fantasy.
I idled in a blue mood.
One glance, and words
Blanched obsolete.
I was the passenger
In her car, without
A seatbelt, hard
To temptation,
Fast to the seat,
Soft to her eternal
Charms, a butterfly
Easily splattered
On her windshield.
Blonde hair served
A joyous poison.
Motors revved,
Spark revived, as
We passed a sign
Along the desert highway:
Curves ahead.
And we drove past Icarus.

HERE I LIE

Here I lie,
Naked,
A vessel
For your
Limbs.
Delicate.
Fragile.
Human.
Touch is
The fabric
We all need.
Sentence me
To pleasure,
Damn me to
An everlasting
Desire for
Sustenance.
Your joints
Fit well into
Mine — these
Words filled
My thoughts
Long ago,
Provided hope
For a dalliance
Never to end.

I still lie bare.
You, gone now,
Deployed in your
Own peep show,
Dazzling the
World with your
Brilliance. Beings
Of light bounce
In another's
Dimension, as I
Please myself,
Sad in this fact:
I guarantee my
Own happiness.
I squawk, leak,
Create residue.
The pastures
At the far side of
My mind float
Like dinghies
On a deep
Ocean, ever more.
I fib horizontal,
And wait for
Kindness to kiss,
My shell, unborn.

ACKNOWLEDGMENTS

First and foremost, thank you to my family (Y, K, and M). And there are many other people who have helped me with these words: Everyone on Light Street; Everyone from *Vanity Fair*; Everyone from *Sports Illustrated*, Lisa P. LeGrand, Andrew Paredes and Family, Jamille McClendon, Jackie Gardner, Robson Garcia, Chilembwe Mason; James Chan, Brian Jaramillo, Hiromi Saeki, Chi Mac, Faisal Azam, Erica Velis, John Plenge, Anne Vallersnes, Paul Gutierrez, Dimitry Léger, Naomi Castillo, Lisa Darling, Karen Lee, Ancel Bowlin, Caryn Prime, Scott Hevesy, Jaramay Aref, Sonja Kiefer, Bettina Meetz, Linda Bukasen, Julia Luu, João Serejo, Kevin Gidden, Claudia Ancalmo (and everyone from Disneyland), Karen Strauss, Edward Sanchez, Cynthia Cortes, Jennymar, Mrs. Pell, Lars Anderson, Tracy Mothershed, Simone Procas, Judy Margolin, Gary Garrison, Andrea Woo, Albert Chen, Bob Der, Jordan Bell, Mike Johnson, Julian Rozzell Jr., the cast and crew of all my independent films, Seevon Chau and family, Marina and Jason Anderson of Polgarus Studio, Everyone at the Minskoff Theater, everyone at St. Matthias, Willie Joe Philbin and The Philbin Family, my friends, fraternity brothers and football teammates at the University of Arizona, my classmates at NYU. If I have forgotten anyone, it was not intentional.

Kelvin C. Bias, New York City, July 2024

OTHER WORK BY
KELVIN C. BIAS

MILKMAN (Novel)

What happens when everyman Calder Boyd starts to lactate? The Manhattanite becomes a media cause célèbre nicknamed the Milkman and old and new problems spill forth. The son of a former NBA star and a Norwegian artist, Calder copes with his strained marriage, losing his copywriting job at a boutique ad agency, a male-empowerment espousing mailman and a porn-star performance artist who wants to exploit him. He also deals with his late father's legacy and his wife's past indiscretion—all while breastfeeding their newborn daughter. Calder eventually becomes a pawn in the battle between a feminist organization and a militant men's society as he tries to become a better husband and man. The Fourth Estate, sex, art, love, memory, marriage and family converge during the snowiest winter on record in this commentary on contemporary American fatherhood.

WHISPERS OF A DYING SUN (Poetry)

These poems represent the vestiges of man from the perspective of a distant future. Akin to radio signals, the remnants of humanity streak toward a black hole where art, politics, love, technology, philosophy, science and the yearning for eternity accrete. Prophetic, stoic, polyphasic, the words disassemble and recombine on the other side in search of a new sun. I hope these poems find a closer home in your personal universe, heard but you're unsure of their origin, like whispers.

SEXOPOLIS: POEMS ON LOVE AND SEX

Love is a liberation, an act, a rebellion, a restriction, a communion. This poetry collection covers the universal topics of love and sex. From erotic to platonic and from marital to familial, love comes in many forms. We don't always get it, but we all crave it.

IMMACULATE DUST: LOVE POEMS

This poetry collection delves headlong into the world of love. Encompassing the realms of dream, fantasy and reality, the poems intend to engender not just love, but more pointedly, lovemaking. Lust. Love. Languor. These are three states of mind and body before, during and after the most pleasant poetry of human interaction: consented sex. We all possess desire, and we are all made of dust. Immaculate dust.

21 PARTICLES OF ETERNITY (Poetry)

Is eternity a quantifiable entity? An existence that can be divided into smaller particles, assembled and disassembled like a puzzle? Can it be bent? Borrowed? Recycled? Eternity is elusive. It constantly seems beyond our grasp yet always within our reach. *21 Particles of Eternity* covers topics as disparate as Mars and pornography, and ranging from global warming and parenthood to politics and death. The poet posits this: perhaps there are hidden portals where eternity can be glimpsed for fleeting moments, and the quest to find them brings meaning. How many particles will you find?

IF THE SKY IS AWAKE (Poetry)

Why do we have a 24-hour day, 60-minute hour, and 60-second minute? Thank the ancient Egyptians, Sumerians and Babylonians. Going further back, in humanity's early days, time was simply measured by the interval between sunrise and sunset. Today, we have much more precise methods. One second is defined as the duration of 9,192,631,770 periods of the radiation corresponding to the transition between the two hyperfine levels of the ground state of a cesium 133 atom. Confusing? Yes. Sometimes what transpires in daylight is the purest. Each day is a new dawn, a chance to reinvent yourself, find new love, rekindle an old one, and peer into the sky and feel awake. Reading poetry is like living life by your own clock. Lose yourself in your own sky.

THE LAST WILL & TESTAMENT OF THE UNITED STATES OF AMERICA: POETRY

This poetry collection conveys my anger and sadness over the current state of America—black, brown, yellow, red, white, and blue. On May 25, 2020—Memorial Day—a white woman named Amy Cooper walked her dog without a required leash in an area of Central Park known as the Ramble, and Christian Cooper, a peaceful, bird-watching black man, asked her to leash her dog. The legacy of slavery writ-large in the astounding fact they had the same surname. Amy responded by calling 911 to say that "an African-

ABOUT THE AUTHOR

Kelvin C. Bias is a journalist, novelist, poet, filmmaker, and raconteur. However, his most important moniker is father. He holds a B.A. in Political Science from the University of Arizona and an M.F.A in Screenwriting from NYU. He lives in New York City with his family.

Nude Blue is his 11th poetry collection. Connect with Kelvin on Instagram: @ArchiveZero